AF258974

AI for Accountants: Tools, Trends and Transformations

Steven M. Bragg

ISBN 978-1-64221-332-4

For more information about AccountingTools® products, visit our Web site at www.accountingtools.com.

Table of Contents

About the Author

Steven Bragg, CPA, has been the chief financial officer or controller of four companies, as well as a consulting manager at Ernst & Young. He received a master's degree in finance from Bentley College, an MBA from Babson College, and a Bachelor's degree in Economics from the University of Maine. He has been a two-time president of the Colorado Mountain Club, and is an avid alpine skier, mountain biker, and certified master diver. Mr. Bragg resides in Centennial, Colorado. He has written more than 300 books and courses, including *New Controller Guidebook*, *GAAP Guidebook*, and *Payroll Management*. He has also written *The Auditors* science fiction trilogy.

Steven maintains the accountingtools.com web site, which contains continuing professional education courses, the Accounting Best Practices podcast, and thousands of articles on accounting subjects.

Buy Additional AccountingTools Courses

AccountingTools offers more than 1,500 hours of CPE courses, with concentrations in accounting, auditing, finance, taxation, and ethics. Related courses that you might like include:

- Accounting Best Practices
- Lean Accounting Guidebook
- New Controller Guidebook

Go to accountingtools.com/cpe to view these additional courses.

AI for Accountants

Introduction

Artificial intelligence is transforming the accounting profession, reshaping traditional workflows, and redefining the role of accountants in a data-driven world. This manual introduces professionals to the foundational principles of AI and explores its practical applications across key accounting functions, including transaction processing, auditing, financial reporting, tax compliance, and fraud detection. Through real-world case studies and explanations of emerging technologies, this manual equips accountants with the knowledge to become more efficient and effective in their jobs.

Overview of Artificial Intelligence and its Evolution

Artificial Intelligence (AI) refers to the simulation of human intelligence processes by computer systems. These processes include learning (acquiring data and rules for using it), reasoning (using rules to reach approximate or definite conclusions), and self-correction. AI systems range from narrow applications like voice assistants and recommendation engines to advanced systems capable of learning and making decisions independently.

The formal foundation for AI was laid in the 1950s, when British mathematician Alan Turing proposed the idea of a machine that could simulate any human intelligence task—a concept later formalized in his famous Turing Test. In 1956, the term "Artificial Intelligence" was coined at the Dartmouth Conference, marking the official birth of AI as a field of study.

Early progress in AI during the 1950s and 1960s led to the development of rule-based systems and simple problem-solving programs. Researchers were optimistic, expecting rapid progress toward human-like intelligence. However, limited computational power and a lack of data soon led to the first "AI winter" in the 1970s, a period of reduced funding and interest. The 1980s saw a resurgence in AI, primarily through expert systems that encoded domain-specific knowledge into rules. While successful in areas like medical diagnosis, these systems were brittle and difficult to scale. Another slowdown followed in the late 1980s and early 1990s.

A major turning point came in the late 1990s and 2000s with the rise of machine learning, a subset of AI that enables systems to learn patterns from data. This shift was fueled by increased computing power, large-scale data availability, and algorithmic advances. Notably, IBM's Deep Blue defeated chess champion Garry Kasparov in 1997, showcasing the potential of AI in complex decision-making.

The 2010s witnessed the explosion of deep learning, a form of machine learning that uses neural networks with many layers. Breakthroughs in image recognition, speech processing, and natural language understanding emerged, powered by technologies like convolutional neural networks and recurrent neural networks. AI became mainstream, enabling innovations like autonomous vehicles, language translation, and intelligent personal assistants (e.g., Siri, Alexa).

Today, AI encompasses a broad range of technologies, including computer vision, natural language processing (NLP), robotics, and reinforcement learning. Tools like ChatGPT demonstrate the power of large language models trained on massive datasets, capable of generating human-like text, answering questions, and even coding.

Looking forward, AI's trajectory is expected to advance toward general intelligence, systems capable of understanding and learning any intellectual task a human can perform. While true artificial general intelligence (AGI) remains a long-term goal, ongoing innovations suggest that AI will continue transforming industries, economies, and daily life across the globe.

Key Artificial Intelligence Terms

A full set of terms related to artificial intelligence is located in the glossary near the end of this manual. In addition, we have noted a few essential terms in this section that are critical to one's understanding of how artificial intelligence systems function. They are as follows:

- *Machine learning.* A subset of AI that enables computers to learn from data without being explicitly programmed. Machine learning algorithms use statistical techniques to identify patterns and improve their performance on a task over time.
- *Deep learning.* A specialized branch of machine learning that uses multi-layered neural networks to model complex patterns in large datasets. Deep learning is especially effective in areas such as image recognition, speech processing, and natural language understanding.
- *Natural language processing.* A field of AI that enables machines to understand, interpret, and generate human language. NLP powers applications like chatbots, machine translation, sentiment analysis, and voice-activated assistants.

Why AI Matters in Accounting

Artificial intelligence is transforming the accounting profession by automating repetitive tasks, enhancing accuracy, and enabling deeper insights into financial data. As businesses increasingly generate large volumes of financial information, AI provides the tools necessary to handle, analyze, and derive value from this data efficiently and reliably.

One of the most significant contributions of AI in accounting is automation. Routine tasks such as data entry, invoice processing, bank reconciliations, and expense management can now be performed by AI-driven systems with minimal human intervention. This not only reduces the risk of human error but also significantly improves the speed and consistency of accounting operations. For example, AI-powered optical character recognition tools can extract relevant data from physical or digital documents, eliminating the need for manual input.

AI also enhances the accuracy and reliability of financial records. Machine learning algorithms can identify anomalies, detect fraud, and flag unusual transactions by comparing real-time data to historical patterns. This continuous monitoring capability strengthens internal controls and helps ensure compliance with financial regulations. Auditors, too, benefit from AI tools that can quickly analyze vast datasets to uncover discrepancies, outliers, or trends that merit further investigation, increasing the effectiveness and efficiency of audit procedures.

Another key advantage of AI is its ability to generate insights and support decision-making. Through advanced analytics and predictive modeling, AI systems can identify trends, forecast future financial performance, and simulate the impact of different business scenarios. For instance, CFOs can use AI to model cash flow projections under various market conditions, enabling more informed strategic planning. These insights allow finance professionals to shift from traditional record-keeping roles to strategic advisors who contribute to value creation.

Natural language processing, a subset of AI, further enhances communication and reporting within accounting. NLP enables systems to understand and generate human language, facilitating the creation of narrative reports from numerical data. This technology allows for the development of intelligent assistants that can answer accounting queries, summarize financial results, or draft regulatory filings.

While AI brings significant benefits, its adoption also raises important considerations. Accountants must understand AI's capabilities and limitations, ensure data integrity, and address ethical concerns such as bias and transparency in automated decision-making. Additionally, as AI handles more transactional tasks, accounting professionals must develop new skills in data analysis, systems integration, and strategic advisory services to remain competitive.

In conclusion, AI matters in accounting because it enhances efficiency, accuracy, and strategic value. By automating routine processes, detecting errors and fraud, and providing actionable insights, AI allows accountants to focus on higher-value activities. As the technology continues to evolve, its role in shaping the future of the accounting profession will only grow more critical.

Ethical and Regulatory Considerations

The integration of artificial intelligence into accounting has brought transformative benefits, including automation, accuracy, and analytical power. However, it also introduces a range of ethical and regulatory challenges that must be addressed to ensure its responsible use. As AI tools increasingly influence financial decisions, auditors' judgments, and compliance efforts, accountants and regulators must evaluate how these systems align with professional standards, privacy requirements, and societal expectations. The following issues must be considered:

- *Internal logic is not obvious.* Many AI models, particularly those based on deep learning, function as "black boxes," meaning their internal logic is not easily understandable. This lack of explainability poses problems in accounting, where stakeholders must justify and trace financial decisions. If an AI system makes an erroneous tax classification or mis-flags a legitimate transaction as fraudulent, understanding the rationale behind the decision is critical. Without transparency, such decisions cannot be effectively reviewed or audited.

- *AI bias.* AI models learn from historical data, which may reflect past human prejudices or structural inequalities. For example, if a machine learning algorithm used for credit risk assessment is trained on biased data, it could inadvertently favor or disadvantage certain groups, potentially violating ethical and legal standards. Accountants must ensure that data used in AI models is representative, fair, and regularly tested for unintended bias.

- *Conflict with data privacy laws.* Accounting involves sensitive financial information that must be handled securely. AI systems require access to large datasets, increasing the risk of data breaches or misuse. Compliance with regulations such as the General Data Protection Regulation (GDPR) in Europe or the California Consumer Privacy Act (CCPA) in the U.S. is essential. These laws mandate safeguards around data collection, processing, and the rights of individuals to access or delete their information.

- *Lack of regulatory guidelines.* There is currently a gap between the pace of AI development and the establishment of formal guidelines. Accounting standards bodies and regulatory agencies are beginning to respond. For instance, the International Ethics Standards Board for Accountants (IESBA) has emphasized the importance of maintaining integrity, objectivity, and professional competence in AI-augmented environments. However, existing regulations often do not explicitly address AI, creating uncertainty around accountability when automated decisions lead to errors or violations.

- *Auditability concerns.* Accountants must ensure that AI-driven processes are fully auditable, with logs, version histories, and validation protocols in place. Regulators may require documentation of how AI models are developed, tested, and maintained, particularly in publicly traded companies or those in regulated industries.

In conclusion, while AI brings significant advantages to accounting, it must be governed by ethical principles and regulatory oversight to ensure its responsible use. As AI continues to evolve, ongoing collaboration between accountants, technologists, and regulators will be necessary to create frameworks that uphold public trust and maintain the integrity of the accounting profession.

We will expand upon these basic conceptual issues through the remainder of this manual.

The Foundations of AI Technologies

It is impossible to understand how artificial intelligence functions, or its impact on the accounting function, without delving into the basics of machine learning, natural language processing, data types, and AI model training. We cover these concepts in the following sub-sections.

The Basics of Machine Learning

Machine learning is a subset of artificial intelligence that is focused on the development of algorithms that allow computers to learn from and make predictions or decisions based on data. Instead of being explicitly programmed to perform tasks, machine learning systems identify patterns in data and use those patterns to inform future behavior. There are three main types of machine learning: supervised learning, unsupervised learning, and reinforcement learning.

Supervised learning is the most commonly used form of machine learning. In this approach, the algorithm is trained on a labeled dataset, which means that each training example is paired with the correct output. The model learns to map inputs to the correct outputs by identifying patterns in the data. Supervised learning is used in applications like email spam detection, credit scoring, and image classification. For instance, in a spam filter, the model is shown examples of emails that are marked as "spam" or "not spam" and learns to classify future emails accordingly. Common algorithms used include linear regression, decision trees, support vector machines, and neural networks.

Unsupervised learning, in contrast, works with data that has no labeled outcomes. The system tries to learn the structure of the data by identifying patterns, groupings, or associations within it. One well-known application is customer segmentation, where a retailer may want to group customers into segments based on purchasing behavior without knowing in advance how many segments exist or what defines them. Algorithms commonly used for unsupervised learning include k-means clustering, hierarchical clustering, and principal component analysis. These techniques are also useful for anomaly detection, such as identifying fraudulent transactions or equipment failures.

Reinforcement learning is a different paradigm in which an agent learns to make decisions by interacting with an environment. The agent takes actions and receives feedback in the form of rewards or penalties. Over time, it learns a policy that maximizes the cumulative reward. Reinforcement learning is inspired by behavioral psychology and is often used in robotics, game playing, and real-time decision-making. A classic example is training a computer to play chess or Go. The agent is not told the correct moves but learns by playing games and receiving feedback on its performance.

Each of these learning types has unique strengths and is suited to different kinds of problems. Supervised learning is highly effective when historical labeled data is available. Unsupervised learning helps in uncovering hidden patterns or intrinsic structures within data. Reinforcement learning is ideal for environments where decisions need to be made sequentially with long-term outcomes in mind. In practice, machine learning often combines elements from these categories. For example, semi-supervised learning uses a mix of labeled and unlabeled data, while deep reinforcement learning combines neural networks with reinforcement techniques. As machine learning continues to evolve, its ability to adapt to diverse problems ensures its central role in the development of intelligent systems.

Natural Language Processing and Computer Vision in Accounting

Natural language processing (NLP) and computer vision (CV) are two powerful sub-fields of artificial intelligence that are increasingly transforming the accounting profession. They enable machines to interpret and process unstructured data, both text and images, thereby automating complex, time-consuming tasks that are traditionally performed by accountants.

Natural language processing focuses on the interaction between computers and human language. In accounting, NLP is primarily used to extract, understand, and analyze information from textual data such as financial reports, contracts, emails, and regulatory filings. One of the most significant applications is the automation of document reviews. For instance, NLP can quickly process and interpret lease agreements to extract key terms such as payment obligations, renewal dates, and interest rates. This significantly reduces the time required for compliance with accounting standards like ASC 842 (Leases).

Another use of NLP is in sentiment analysis of financial statements, earnings calls, or news articles to assess the tone and detect potential financial risks. NLP algorithms can also power intelligent chatbots used in financial customer service or employee support functions, answering routine queries about expenses, policies, or compliance. Additionally, *natural language generation* (NLG), a branch of NLP, can create narrative reports summarizing financial data for stakeholders, turning raw figures into clear, readable commentary.

Computer vision enables computers to interpret and process visual information such as images or scanned documents. In accounting, CV is commonly used for automating data extraction from physical documents. For example, invoices, receipts, bank statements, and tax forms—often received as scanned images or PDFs—can be digitized and processed using optical character recognition combined with CV algorithms. This allows the system to locate, extract, and classify relevant information such as dates, totals, vendor names, and tax IDs.

Computer vision is particularly beneficial in expense management systems, where employees can upload pictures of receipts and have the system automatically categorize and enter the data into the accounting software. In audits, CV can be used to compare scanned copies of invoices and purchase orders to detect discrepancies, verify authenticity, or identify potential fraud. The technology also assists in fixed asset tracking by recognizing barcodes, QR codes, or visual features of assets in inventory audits.

The integration of NLP and CV enhances the automation of end-to-end accounting processes. For instance, in accounts payable, CV captures and interprets invoice images, NLP extracts key data, and machine learning validates and posts the entries. This seamless integration leads to improved accuracy, faster processing, and reduced operational costs.

As regulatory and financial documentation grows in volume and complexity, NLP and CV allow accountants to focus on analysis and strategic insight rather than manual data entry and validation. NLP and computer vision are vital tools in modernizing accounting workflows.

Data Types Used in AI Applications

Artificial intelligence applications in accounting rely heavily on diverse data types to deliver insights, perform automation, and improve decision-making. Understanding the kinds of data involved is essential to building effective AI systems. In accounting, these data types can be broadly categorized into structured, unstructured, semi-structured, and time-series data, each playing a distinct role in AI applications.

Structured data is the most traditional and widely used in accounting. It is highly organized and easily stored in databases or spreadsheets, typically in rows and columns. Examples include general ledger entries, trial balances, journal entries, accounts receivable and payable data, payroll records, tax filings, and inventory records. Because structured data is numeric and categorical (e.g., invoice numbers, amounts, dates), it is ideal for AI techniques such as supervised learning and statistical analysis. These applications include automated reconciliations, predictive analytics for cash flow forecasting, and anomaly detection in audit procedures.

Unstructured data refers to information that lacks a predefined data model. In accounting, unstructured data includes scanned receipts, contracts, email communications, audit working papers, and PDF reports. AI models using natural language processing and computer vision extract insights from this data. For instance, NLP can process lease agreements to extract payment terms, while computer vision tools can analyze scanned invoices for transaction details. This data type is especially important for compliance automation, audit documentation review, and fraud detection where manual interpretation would otherwise be required.

Semi-structured data has elements of both structured and unstructured data. It does not fit neatly into tables but still contains tags or markers to separate data elements. Examples in accounting include XML or JSON files used in financial reporting systems, e-invoicing systems, or tax filings. For instance, XBRL (eXtensible Business Reporting Language), widely used for SEC financial filings, is a semi-structured format. AI tools can parse these formats to automate the extraction, mapping, and comparison of financial information, enabling efficient benchmarking and regulatory compliance checks.

Time-series data is a specific type of structured data that tracks variables over time. In accounting, this includes data such as monthly revenue, daily cash balances, stock prices, and expense trends. Time-series analysis is crucial for forecasting and trend analysis. AI models trained on historical financial data can predict future cash flows, detect seasonal fluctuations, or identify unusual trends that may signal risk or opportunity.

Each of these data types enables specific AI capabilities in accounting, from document automation and risk scoring to predictive insights and real-time anomaly detection. The effectiveness of AI in accounting hinges not only on algorithm quality but also on the relevance, accuracy, and integration of these data types. As AI adoption accelerates, the ability to harmonize and leverage diverse data types will be a critical skill for accounting professionals.

AI Model Training and Accuracy Considerations

Training an artificial intelligence model for use in accounting involves several critical steps that ensure the model delivers accurate, reliable, and relevant results. The accounting department deals with high-stakes data, so precision in AI performance is essential. The success of AI applications in accounting hinges not only on the sophistication of the model but also on the quality of the data used for training and the measures taken to evaluate and improve accuracy.

Model training begins with the collection of representative data. For accounting purposes, this includes general ledger entries, journal transactions, invoices, payroll records, tax filings, and audit logs. The training dataset must be clean, complete, and properly labeled, particularly for supervised learning models. For example, a model designed to flag fraudulent transactions must be trained on historical transactions labeled as "fraudulent" or "legitimate." If the data is inconsistent, contains errors, or lacks sufficient diversity, the model will learn incorrect patterns, leading to poor performance.

Preprocessing is another key step in accounting model training. This may involve normalizing financial figures, encoding categorical values like account codes, or extracting entities from scanned documents using optical character recognition. For natural language processing tasks, such as contract analysis or sentiment analysis of financial reports, the text data must be cleaned, and formatted consistently.

Model selection depends on the accounting task at hand. For example, classification models may be used for transaction categorization, regression models for forecasting cash flows, and clustering algorithms for identifying spending patterns. Deep learning may be applied to more complex tasks such as interpreting scanned receipts or analyzing unstructured narratives in audit documents.

Accuracy considerations are paramount. In accounting, false positives (e.g., flagging a valid invoice as fraudulent) can create operational delays, while false negatives (missing actual errors) can lead to compliance issues or financial loss. Therefore, a variety of performance metrics are used to evaluate models, especially when dealing with imbalanced datasets common in fraud detection or error classification.

To maintain high accuracy, ongoing model evaluation and retraining are necessary. Accounting environments are dynamic, since new regulations, business processes, and data formats emerge frequently. Without continuous updates, an AI model may become outdated and unreliable. Feedback loops, where human accountants review and correct AI predictions, are vital for reinforcing learning and improving performance over time.

Another important aspect is explainability. Given the regulatory and audit-heavy nature of accounting, stakeholders must understand how an AI model arrived at its conclusions. Models that are black boxes, such as some deep learning architectures, may be inappropriate for critical accounting functions unless supported by interpretability tools or techniques.

In summary, training AI models for accounting requires meticulous data preparation, rigorous accuracy testing, and continuous refinement. The accounting department must collaborate closely with data scientists to ensure that AI tools are both technically sound and aligned with financial reporting, compliance, and audit standards. Properly trained and validated models can enhance efficiency, accuracy, and insight within the accounting function.

Automation in Transactional Accounting

Artificial intelligence is transforming core functions in the accounting department, particularly data entry, invoice processing, and reconciliations. These traditionally manual tasks are often time-consuming, error-prone, and repetitive, making them prime candidates for AI-driven automation.

In the realm of data entry, AI systems are used to automate the capture and input of financial data from various sources. Rather than relying on manual typing or basic templates, AI can extract relevant details from structured documents like spreadsheets or unstructured ones such as emails, receipts, or scanned images. Through NLP and optical character recognition, the technology can interpret and categorize information, converting it into usable digital data. Machine learning models improve accuracy over time by learning from corrections and adapting to different formats. This not only speeds up data entry but also reduces the risk of human error and ensures more reliable financial records.

Invoice processing is another area where AI provides substantial benefits. Traditional invoice processing involves receiving invoices in various formats, validating them against purchase orders and delivery receipts, and manually entering details into an accounting system. AI streamlines this workflow by reading invoice contents using OCR and NLP, verifying data against internal records, flagging discrepancies, and initiating approval workflows. Some AI systems also learn an organization's payment policies and vendor terms to ensure timely and compliant payments. As a result, invoice cycle times are shortened, duplicate or fraudulent invoices can be detected, and staff are freed up to focus on exceptions and strategic tasks.

Reconciliations are a critical but tedious accounting function. AI enhances the reconciliation process by automatically comparing bank statements, ledgers, and supporting documents to identify matches and flag discrepancies. Advanced algorithms can detect subtle anomalies, such as timing differences or partial payments, and suggest likely matches that a human might overlook. Furthermore, AI systems can continuously learn from reconciled transactions to refine their logic, making the process more accurate and efficient over time. In high-volume environments, such as large enterprises or financial institutions, this significantly reduces the workload on accounting staff and accelerates month-end or year-end closing activities.

The use of AI in these three accounting functions not only increases operational efficiency but also improves compliance and decision-making. By automating routine tasks, AI reduces the likelihood of regulatory or reporting errors and provides a clear audit trail. Additionally, it allows accountants to focus on higher-value activities such as financial analysis, forecasting, and strategic planning.

AI vs. Robotic Process Automation

Robotic process automation (RPA) is a technology that uses software robots to automate highly repetitive and rule-based tasks within business processes. In accounting, RPA can handle activities such as data extraction, invoice processing, and reconciliations, reducing manual effort and minimizing errors. It operates by mimicking human interactions with digital systems, but does so faster and more consistently.

AI and RPA serve distinct yet complementary roles. RPA focuses on automating rule-based, repetitive tasks such as invoice processing, bank reconciliations, and data entry, increasing speed and accuracy without altering the underlying logic. In contrast, AI adds a layer of intelligence by analyzing patterns, learning from data, and making decisions—such as identifying anomalies in transactions, predicting cash flows, or interpreting unstructured documents like contracts. While RPA is ideal for structured tasks with clear rules, AI is better suited for complex, judgment-based processes that benefit from adaptability and continuous learning.

CASE STUDY

Coca-Cola Bottling Company United (CCBCU), one of the largest privately held Coca-Cola bottlers in the United States, faced significant operational challenges in its accounts payable (AP) department. The company processed over 50,000 invoices per month across multiple locations, relying heavily on manual data entry and paper-based approvals. This created bottlenecks, increased the risk of human error, and limited the payables team's ability to manage vendor relationships and control cash flow efficiently.

To address these issues, CCBCU implemented an AI-driven AP automation solution from Kofax, which used intelligent document processing, machine learning, and robotic process automation (RPA). The solution was designed to capture, classify, and extract data from both paper and electronic invoices, while also validating information against purchase orders and vendor records within the company's enterprise resource planning (ERP) system.

The AI platform significantly improved the speed and accuracy of invoice processing. Using OCR and machine learning, the system automatically recognized and extracted relevant fields from invoices, regardless of formatting differences across vendors. Over time, it learned to improve data extraction accuracy based on feedback from the AP staff. Additionally, RPA bots were deployed to match invoices to purchase orders and receipts, route them for approvals, and post them directly into the ERP system.

The results were impressive. Invoice processing times were reduced by over 70%, and manual data entry was virtually eliminated. The AP team was able to reallocate time from routine tasks to exception handling, vendor communication, and strategic analysis. The company also reported a significant reduction in late payment penalties and an increase in early payment discounts, improving both cash flow and vendor satisfaction.

Furthermore, the AI system provided real-time reporting and analytics, giving CCBCU's finance leaders better visibility into liabilities and cash position. This transparency supported improved decision-making and tighter control over corporate spending.

In summary, Coca-Cola Bottling Company United's implementation of AI-driven accounts payable automation transformed its financial operations. By eliminating manual processes and leveraging intelligent automation, the company achieved faster cycle times, higher accuracy, and greater operational efficiency. The success of this project illustrates the growing value of AI technologies in modernizing accounting workflows and enhancing overall financial performance.

AI in Financial Reporting and Analysis

Artificial intelligence is playing a growing role in automating the generation of financial statements, which offers significant benefits in speed, accuracy, and insight. Traditionally, financial statement preparation has required extensive manual data aggregation, validation, and formatting. With AI, this process can be streamlined using intelligent systems that extract, analyze, and compile financial data from multiple sources to produce financial statements and related disclosures with minimal human intervention.

AI-powered tools can collect financial data from ERP systems, general ledgers, bank feeds, and subledgers, such as accounts payable and receivable. Through machine learning algorithms and natural language processing, these tools can understand financial classifications, interpret transactional data, and map it to the correct financial statement line items. For example, AI can distinguish between capital expenditures and operating expenses based on patterns in past entries or metadata attached to invoices. This automation ensures that financial statements are not only prepared faster but also in compliance with relevant accounting standards.

One of the key advantages of using AI in financial statement preparation is real-time reporting. Rather than waiting for end-of-period closing activities, businesses can generate up-to-date financial statements on demand. This capability is particularly useful for management teams and investors seeking current insights into a company's performance and financial health. AI systems can continuously monitor financial transactions and update the relevant portions of financial statements automatically, enabling more proactive financial management.

AI also enhances accuracy by reducing the potential for human error. In traditional processes, mistakes can occur during manual data entry, spreadsheet consolidation, or journal entry posting. AI systems, by contrast, apply predefined logic consistently and flag anomalies that might indicate data entry errors, duplicate transactions, or missing entries. These systems can also detect inconsistencies across accounts or between internal and external reports, such as bank statements and general ledger entries.

Furthermore, AI tools can support disclosure preparation and narrative analysis. Using NLP, AI can draft the text that accompanies financial statements, such as management discussion and analysis sections or footnotes, based on financial results and trends. These tools can describe revenue movements, highlight significant variances, and summarize financial risks, providing context alongside the numbers. While human review is still essential to ensure accuracy and regulatory compliance, the use of AI significantly reduces the time and effort involved.

The use of AI in financial statement preparation is particularly beneficial for large organizations, multinational corporations, and entities with complex operations. These organizations often face time pressure at quarter-end or year-end closings, and AI helps to expedite reporting cycles. Additionally, smaller companies and accounting firms are adopting AI-based platforms to improve efficiency and offer clients more timely financial information.

In conclusion, AI is revolutionizing the generation of financial statements by automating data processing, enhancing accuracy, enabling real-time reporting, and supporting narrative generation. While AI does not replace the need for professional judgment, it serves as a powerful tool that enables accounting teams to shift their focus from manual compilation to higher-value activities like financial analysis and strategic planning.

CASE STUDY

Microsoft leveraged artificial intelligence to transform its financial reporting processes, addressing the complexity and scale of managing financial data across hundreds of subsidiaries in more than 190 countries. With its rapid growth and numerous business units, Microsoft faced significant challenges in consolidating financial data, ensuring compliance, and producing timely, accurate reports for internal decision-making and external regulatory filings.

To streamline and enhance its financial reporting, Microsoft implemented AI-powered tools within its finance operations, particularly through the use of machine learning and natural language processing. These technologies were integrated into Microsoft's Dynamics 365 and Power BI platforms to automate data validation, detect anomalies, and accelerate the generation of financial statements and disclosures.

One of the key improvements was the use of AI to identify inconsistencies and errors in data submissions from Microsoft's global subsidiaries. By applying machine learning algorithms trained on historical data and reporting rules, the system automatically flagged anomalies such as missing values, unusual account fluctuations, or non-compliant entries. These alerts allowed accounting teams to address issues early in the reporting cycle, reducing the risk of last-minute adjustments and compliance breaches.

Additionally, Microsoft used NLP to automate parts of the narrative commentary required for internal management reports and external disclosures. AI systems could generate draft text that explained variances in performance, highlighted key financial trends, and summarized results. Accountants then reviewed and refined this content, saving considerable time while ensuring consistency in tone and messaging.

The AI-driven solution also enhanced real-time visibility into financial performance. With automated dashboards and analytics powered by AI, Microsoft's accounting managers could access up-to-date reports and drill down into metrics with greater speed and granularity. This enabled more informed, agile decision-making and improved transparency across the organization.

As a result of these initiatives, Microsoft achieved faster reporting cycles, higher data accuracy, and improved compliance with accounting standards. The accounting team was able to shift its focus from manual data preparation to value-added analysis and strategic planning. Furthermore, the integration of AI into financial reporting positioned Microsoft to scale its accounting function effectively as the company continued to grow.

In summary, Microsoft's use of AI in financial reporting illustrates how large, complex organizations can leverage intelligent automation to increase efficiency, reduce errors, and deliver more timely and insightful financial information.

Pattern Recognition and Anomaly Detection

Artificial intelligence has become a vital tool in accounting for pattern recognition and anomaly detection, enabling organizations to monitor vast volumes of financial data with unprecedented speed and accuracy. Traditionally, accountants and auditors relied on manual methods or rule-based systems to identify irregularities, which often limited their ability to uncover complex or subtle issues. With the application of AI, and especially machine learning and data analytics, accounting teams can now detect patterns and anomalies in real time, reducing the risk of fraud, errors, and financial misstatements.

Pattern recognition in accounting involves identifying recurring trends or expected behaviors in financial data. AI algorithms can learn these patterns by analyzing historical transactions, budgetary data, or industry benchmarks. For instance, AI can recognize that a certain vendor is typically paid monthly at a consistent rate, or that sales tend to follow seasonal trends. Once these patterns are established, the system continuously monitors incoming data for deviations. This makes it easier to identify potentially problematic transactions, such as duplicate payments, unexpected spikes in expenses, or uncharacteristic journal entries.

Anomaly detection refers to the identification of outliers or unusual data points that do not conform to expected patterns. In accounting, anomalies can indicate fraud, data entry errors, or operational issues. AI-based anomaly detection models use statistical methods and machine learning techniques to distinguish between normal variation and suspicious activity. For example, if a travel reimbursement request significantly exceeds the norm for a specific employee or department, the AI system can flag it for further investigation. Similarly, it can detect instances where revenues appear inflated or expenses are consistently underreported.

One of the key strengths of AI in this domain is its ability to process large datasets from multiple sources – including bank transactions, general ledger entries, payroll files, and procurement systems – much faster than human auditors. This enables continuous monitoring rather than periodic reviews, allowing organizations to respond to anomalies immediately rather than waiting until the end of a reporting period.

AI also adapts over time. As it processes more data and receives feedback from accountants, the models improve their accuracy in identifying true anomalies and reducing false positives. This self-learning capability enhances the reliability of the system and builds trust among users.

In auditing, AI-driven anomaly detection has proven especially effective. Auditors can apply these tools to full populations of data, rather than relying on sampling methods. This broader scope increases audit quality and reduces the likelihood that material misstatements or fraud will go unnoticed. Regulatory compliance is also strengthened, as AI helps ensure financial reporting accuracy and supports robust internal control frameworks.

In conclusion, AI's use in pattern recognition and anomaly detection is transforming the field of accounting. By identifying unusual transactions and behaviors early, it supports better decision-making, risk management, and financial integrity. As organizations continue to generate increasing volumes of financial data, AI provides the tools necessary to keep pace, improve oversight, and enhance trust in financial information.

Predictive Analytics for Forecasting

Artificial intelligence is reshaping forecasting practices in accounting and finance through the use of predictive analytics. *Predictive analytics* involves using historical data, statistical algorithms, and machine learning techniques to anticipate future outcomes. By integrating AI, organizations can generate highly accurate forecasts related to revenue, cash flow, expenses, and financial performance. This enhanced forecasting capability enables better decision-making, improved resource allocation, and more proactive financial management.

Traditional forecasting methods often rely on spreadsheets, static models, and assumptions based on past performance. These methods can be time-consuming and may not adequately adjust for changing conditions or unexpected variables. In contrast, AI-driven predictive analytics continuously learns from new data and dynamically adjusts its forecasts. By analyzing large volumes of historical and real-time data, AI can identify complex patterns, correlations, and trends that are not immediately visible to human analysts.

One of the most valuable applications of AI in forecasting is in revenue prediction. AI models can examine customer purchasing behavior, seasonal trends, sales pipeline data, and external factors such as economic indicators or market conditions. Based on this information, the system forecasts future sales with greater precision than traditional models. This is especially useful for businesses with high transaction volumes or those affected by rapid market changes.

Similarly, AI is used to forecast cash flow by evaluating payment patterns, customer credit behavior, vendor terms, and expected income. The system identifies trends and outliers to predict when cash will be received or spent, allowing finance teams to anticipate shortages or surpluses and adjust strategies accordingly. This proactive cash flow management is crucial for maintaining liquidity and avoiding disruptions in operations.

Expense forecasting also benefits from AI. Algorithms analyze past spending patterns, supplier behavior, inflation rates, and operational data to project future costs. In manufacturing, for example, AI can factor in variables like production schedules, raw material pricing, and logistics disruptions to forecast total expenses more accurately.

These insights allow management to set more realistic budgets and identify potential cost-saving opportunities in advance.

AI also enhances scenario planning, which is vital for strategic forecasting. Predictive models can simulate multiple "what-if" scenarios, testing the financial impact of changes in pricing, demand, labor costs, or regulatory environments. These simulations help organizations prepare for a range of outcomes and develop more resilient business plans.

Moreover, AI-powered forecasting tools often include visual dashboards that allow decision-makers to interact with the data, explore trends, and understand the rationale behind the predictions. This transparency fosters confidence in the forecasts and supports data-driven strategy development.

In conclusion, AI-driven predictive analytics transforms financial forecasting by increasing both the accuracy of forecasts and the frequency with which they can be compiled. By moving beyond static models to real-time projections, organizations can better navigate uncertainty and capitalize on emerging opportunities.

CASE STUDY

Lufthansa Group, one of the world's largest airline operators, adopted AI-based predictive analytics to transform its budgeting and financial planning processes. Facing the challenge of managing operations across multiple countries, subsidiaries, and business lines, the company needed more accurate forecasting tools to respond to volatile fuel prices, fluctuating passenger demand, and global economic uncertainties. Traditional budgeting methods, reliant on manual data consolidation and static assumptions, often led to outdated forecasts and misaligned resource allocation.

To address these issues, Lufthansa partnered with IBM to implement an AI-powered financial planning platform based on IBM Planning Analytics and Watson AI. This platform utilized machine learning to analyze historical financial data, operational metrics, market trends, and external factors such as fuel costs, currency exchange rates, and geopolitical events. The goal was to enable real-time forecasting and dynamic budgeting that could adapt quickly to changing conditions.

The AI system continuously ingested data from across the airline's operations, including ticket sales, capacity planning, maintenance schedules, and fuel consumption. It then applied advanced statistical models to forecast revenue, expenses, and cash flow across different scenarios. One of the key advantages was the ability to simulate multiple "what-if" scenarios, such as changes in flight capacity or economic downturns, and assess their impact on financial performance.

By automating much of the forecasting process, Lufthansa significantly reduced the time required to prepare budgets. Instead of spending weeks consolidating spreadsheets from various departments, finance teams could focus on analyzing outputs and refining strategies. The predictive analytics engine also helped detect early indicators of deviation from budget, allowing managers to take corrective actions proactively.

Within a year of implementation, Lufthansa reported improved accuracy in its revenue and cost forecasts, especially in complex areas like fuel planning and labor cost estimation. This enabled the company to reallocate resources more effectively, optimize scheduling, and improve profitability. Additionally, finance leaders gained greater confidence in their budgeting assumptions, supported by data-driven insights and transparent forecasting logic.

In conclusion, Lufthansa's use of AI-based predictive analytics revolutionized its budgeting process, making it faster, more responsive, and better aligned with business realities. This case demonstrates how advanced forecasting tools can move budgeting from a backward-looking, manual task to a forward-looking, strategic function in large, data-intensive organizations.

Fraud Detection and Risk Management

One of the best accounting activities to which AI can be applied is the use of fraud detection, since it can automatically search large datasets and spot anomalies that would probably not be identified by a human. We explore this opportunity in the following sub-sections, as well as several regulatory compliance implications of this work.

How AI Detects Irregularities

Artificial intelligence is an excellent tool for detecting irregularities and fraudulent activities. It does so with advanced algorithms, machine learning, and pattern recognition capabilities. Traditional methods of fraud detection typically rely on periodic audits and manual reviews, which are both time-consuming and prone to human error. In contrast, AI systems can monitor vast volumes of financial data in real-time, quickly identifying anomalies that may suggest fraudulent behavior or accounting errors.

One of the primary ways AI detects fraud is through anomaly detection algorithms. These systems learn what constitutes "normal" behavior in accounting transactions based on historical data. Once a baseline is established, AI can flag any transaction that deviates significantly from expected patterns. For example, if an employee consistently processes invoices under a certain dollar amount to avoid managerial approval, AI can detect this pattern and raise alerts. Similarly, sudden changes in vendor payment frequencies, employee expense patterns, or revenue recognition methods can all trigger alerts for further investigation.

Machine learning models can be trained to recognize indicators of known fraud schemes, such as duplicate payments, false billings, inflated expenses, and revenue manipulation. These models continuously improve over time as they are exposed to more data, learning from past instances of fraud to refine their predictive capabilities. Natural language processing further enhances AI's utility by analyzing unstructured data, such as emails, memos, or audit notes, for suspicious language or discussions related to financial misconduct.

AI also supports forensic accounting by automating the analysis of journal entries. It can sift through thousands of ledger entries to identify unusual combinations, such as weekend postings, entries by unauthorized users, or unusually timed adjustments at the close of a reporting period. Additionally, AI tools can cross-reference accounting records with external databases — such as vendor master files, tax records, or bank transactions — to detect discrepancies that may indicate fictitious vendors or shell companies.

Another strength of AI lies in its real-time monitoring capabilities. Unlike traditional audits that occur at fixed intervals, AI systems provide continuous oversight, reducing the window of opportunity for fraudulent activities to go undetected. This proactive approach enables accounting departments to prevent fraud or limit its impact rather than merely reacting after damage is done.

Importantly, AI does not replace human auditors but complements them. By automating the initial screening process and highlighting areas of concern, AI allows auditors and accountants to focus their expertise on investigating high-risk areas. This improves the efficiency and accuracy of internal controls and risk management processes.

In short, AI enhances fraud detection through real-time anomaly detection, machine learning, natural language analysis, and automated forensic tools. By identifying patterns and inconsistencies that humans might overlook, AI enables faster, more accurate, and more comprehensive fraud prevention strategies.

CASE STUDY

Microsoft implemented AI-based tools to strengthen its internal auditing and risk assessment functions. The company deployed machine learning models and anomaly detection algorithms to monitor vast quantities of transactional data across its global operations. One of the key objectives was to identify irregularities in employee expense reporting, vendor billing, and internal accounting records that could indicate potential fraud.

In one case, the AI systems flagged an unusual pattern in employee travel and expense claims. The AI detected a small group of employees submitting travel expenses at an unusually high frequency and in inconsistent geographical patterns that did not align with their job roles. Further investigation revealed that these employees were submitting duplicate and inflated receipts for reimbursement. The AI tool had identified these discrepancies by comparing historical travel data, employee roles, and legitimate travel patterns, allowing the internal audit team to take timely action before the losses escalated.

In another case, the AI systems identified a mismatch between purchase orders and vendor payment data, revealing that several payments were being made to a vendor that had no history of fulfilling services. Upon review, it was discovered that a fictitious vendor had been created by an insider who approved and routed false invoices through the system. The AI tool's ability to cross-reference vendor profiles, detect missing deliverables, and analyze unusual approval workflows helped uncover the fraud scheme, which would have been difficult to detect through traditional manual review.

Through these cases, Microsoft demonstrated how AI can be instrumental in uncovering internal fraud by analyzing patterns, flagging anomalies, and enabling early intervention, and shows how even a large and sophisticated organization can benefit from AI's speed, scalability, and precision in identifying fraudulent activities that might otherwise go unnoticed.

Neural Networks and Anomaly Detection Models

Neural networks and anomaly detection models are two of the most powerful AI tools used to detect irregularities and fraud within a business. They are particularly effective due to their ability to learn from vast datasets, identify complex patterns, and detect subtle deviations that traditional rule-based systems might miss. These technologies are increasingly being deployed in accounting, finance, procurement, and compliance functions to enhance internal controls and mitigate fraud risks.

Neural networks consist of layers of interconnected nodes that process and interpret data. In fraud detection, these networks are trained on historical transactional data that includes both normal and fraudulent activity. Once trained, the neural network can analyze new transactions and determine whether they fit known patterns or deviate in suspicious ways. For example, a neural network might detect inconsistencies in the timing, value, and frequency of vendor payments, suggesting potential invoice fraud or unauthorized transactions.

What makes neural networks particularly effective is their ability to handle non-linear relationships and high-dimensional data. This means they can detect fraud even when the fraudulent behavior is intentionally designed to resemble legitimate activity. In areas such as expense reporting, payroll processing, or revenue recognition, neural networks can detect anomalies that would be undetectable by simple threshold or rule-based methods.

Anomaly detection models, while often simpler in architecture than neural networks, are equally critical in spotting fraud. These models identify data points that deviate significantly from an established baseline. For instance, an anomaly detection model might flag a payment to a new vendor that falls outside the normal range of transaction amounts or occurs outside regular business hours. These anomalies could indicate shell company payments, duplicate invoices, or collusion between employees and vendors.

Both approaches benefit significantly from real-time data processing. When integrated into enterprise systems, they enable continuous monitoring rather than periodic audits. This means fraud can be detected and addressed before it causes significant financial harm. Moreover, these models can be retrained and refined continuously, learning from new types of fraud schemes as they emerge.

In practice, businesses combine neural networks and anomaly detection models to create a multi-layered fraud detection system. For example, banks use them to monitor credit card transactions, while large corporations apply them to audit trails, procurement, and payroll systems. These tools significantly reduce the workload on human auditors by filtering out normal transactions and highlighting only the most suspicious cases for review.

Regulatory Compliance Implications of Using AI in Fraud Detection

The use of artificial intelligence in fraud detection and risk management introduces a set of regulatory compliance implications for businesses to manage. As AI becomes more integrated into core financial processes, regulators, auditors, and stakeholders demand transparency, accountability, and alignment with existing compliance frameworks.

One of the primary regulatory concerns is model transparency and explainability. Many AI models, particularly complex machine learning algorithms like neural networks, are often considered "black boxes" because their internal workings are not easily interpretable. Regulatory bodies such as the Securities and Exchange Commission and European supervisory authorities emphasize the importance of explainable AI to ensure that financial decisions made or influenced by AI can be clearly understood and justified. If an AI system flags a transaction as fraudulent or assigns a risk score, companies must be able to explain how that conclusion was reached – especially when adverse actions, such as account freezes or internal investigations, result from the system's output.

Another compliance challenge is data privacy and protection. AI systems rely on large datasets to function effectively, many of which contain sensitive financial, personal, or transactional data. Regulations like the General Data Protection Regulation in Europe and the California Consumer Privacy Act place strict requirements on how data is collected, processed, stored, and used. Companies must ensure that AI systems used for fraud detection comply with these regulations by employing robust data governance policies, anonymization techniques, and secure data storage protocols.

Bias and fairness are also critical compliance issues. If an AI system is trained on biased historical data, it may produce discriminatory outcomes, such as disproportionately flagging transactions associated with specific demographic or geographic groups. Regulatory bodies increasingly scrutinize the fairness of AI systems, particularly when used in areas like credit scoring, insurance underwriting, and internal investigations. Businesses must implement bias detection and mitigation strategies to ensure compliance with anti-discrimination laws and to protect their reputation.

Furthermore, auditability and documentation are essential for regulatory compliance. Regulators expect companies to maintain detailed records of how AI models are developed, tested, validated, and deployed. This includes documentation of model inputs, performance metrics, training datasets, and update procedures. Regular audits of AI systems help ensure that they continue to function as intended and that any changes to their behavior are well-documented and justifiable.

Lastly, companies must align their AI use with sector-specific regulations. For example, financial institutions must ensure compliance with anti-money laundering rules and Know Your Customer standards. AI models used in these contexts must support regulatory reporting requirements, such as generating suspicious activity reports and maintaining appropriate audit trails.

In summary, while AI enhances fraud detection and risk management, it also introduces significant regulatory compliance considerations. Transparency, privacy, fairness, auditability, and adherence to sector-specific rules must be prioritized. By addressing these concerns, organizations can leverage AI effectively while maintaining trust, ethical integrity, and regulatory alignment.

AI in Audit Procedures

There are several possible uses for AI within the field of auditing. As discussed in the following pages, these uses include the automation of audit sampling, risk assessments, and the examination of of contracts and other documentation.

The Automation of Audit Sampling and Risk Assessments

Artificial intelligence is revolutionizing the fields of audit sampling and risk assessment by automating processes that were traditionally manual, time-consuming, and sample-based. By integrating AI into these areas, auditors can significantly enhance the accuracy, efficiency, and coverage of audits, allowing for more data-driven and risk-focused assurance activities.

In traditional auditing, sampling is used to test a subset of transactions under the assumption that it is representative of the entire population. However, this approach has limitations, particularly when fraud or errors are isolated and not evenly distributed. AI addresses this issue by enabling auditors to analyze entire datasets rather than relying on limited samples. Using machine learning and data analytics, AI systems can scan 100% of transactions to identify unusual patterns or anomalies, effectively eliminating the need for random sampling and increasing the likelihood of detecting irregularities.

AI-powered audit sampling is often referred to as *intelligent sampling*. Instead of selecting samples at random, AI evaluates each transaction's characteristics and assigns a risk score based on predefined criteria and learned behaviors. For example, transactions that occur outside business hours, involve new vendors, or exceed certain thresholds can be flagged as high-risk. The auditor can then focus their review efforts on transactions that present the greatest potential for misstatement or fraud, resulting in a more efficient and targeted audit process.

In the area of risk assessment, AI enhances the auditor's ability to identify and evaluate risks early in the audit cycle. Machine learning models analyze historical financial and operational data to uncover risk indicators that may not be obvious through manual analysis. These indicators might include recurring journal entries near period-end, inconsistencies in revenue recognition, or unusual vendor behavior. Natural language processing can also be used to analyze unstructured data sources such as emails, meeting notes, and contracts, providing insights into operational risks and compliance issues.

AI systems can also adapt to changes over time. As they are exposed to more audit engagements and outcomes, these systems continuously learn which risk factors are most predictive of errors or fraud. This dynamic learning capability enables auditors to refine their risk assessment models and improve audit planning from one engagement to the next.

In practice, firms such as Deloitte and KPMG have adopted AI in their audit processes through proprietary platforms that automate sampling and risk assessments.

These systems integrate with client enterprise systems to extract and analyze data continuously, allowing auditors to monitor financial activity in real time rather than waiting for scheduled audit periods.

In short, AI significantly enhances the effectiveness of audit sampling and risk assessments by replacing random, manual processes with comprehensive, intelligent analysis. By automating data review and focusing auditor attention on high-risk areas, AI not only improves audit quality but also provides greater assurance to stakeholders in an increasingly complex financial environment.

CASE STUDY

Deloitte has integrated artificial intelligence into its audit processes through its proprietary platform called Cortex. This AI-powered tool is designed to automate and enhance key audit functions, including data analysis, risk assessment, and anomaly detection. Cortex plays a central role in transforming Deloitte's audit approach from a traditional, sample-based methodology to a data-driven and continuous auditing model.

Cortex connects directly to a client's enterprise resource planning systems, extracting large volumes of financial data in real-time. Once the data is ingested, the platform uses machine learning algorithms to analyze transactions across the general ledger, subledgers, and supporting documentation. It evaluates each transaction against established benchmarks and patterns learned from previous audits. Transactions that deviate from these norms are flagged for further review, allowing auditors to focus on high-risk areas.

A notable use case involved a global consumer goods client where Deloitte deployed Cortex to analyze over 10 million transactions. Traditionally, only a small sample of these transactions would have been tested due to time and resource constraints. With Cortex, Deloitte was able to evaluate the entire dataset, applying advanced anomaly detection to identify irregular entries. These included unusual manual journal entries near quarter-end and duplicate vendor payments, which were potential indicators of financial misstatements or process control issues.

Another key feature of Cortex is its integration of natural language processing, which allows the tool to review textual data such as invoice descriptions, contract terms, and narrative explanations. This capability helped Deloitte uncover compliance issues related to revenue recognition and contract obligations, further improving audit assurance.

Cortex also contributes to real-time risk assessment. By continuously analyzing data, it updates risk profiles throughout the audit cycle, allowing for dynamic audit planning. This adaptability leads to more precise audit procedures and better resource allocation.

In summary, Deloitte's Cortex exemplifies how AI can transform the audit process. It automates data analysis, enhances risk identification, and enables full-population testing—all of which contribute to a more accurate and insightful audit.

The Use of Natural Language Processing to Review Contracts and Documentation

Natural language processing is playing an increasingly important role in the review of contracts and business documentation. NLP helps streamline document analysis, reduce human error, and uncover insights that may otherwise go unnoticed.

One of the key uses of NLP in contract review is clause extraction and classification. Contracts often contain thousands of words, with specific clauses buried deep within long documents. NLP models can be trained to identify and extract critical components such as payment terms, termination clauses, indemnities, confidentiality agreements, and dispute resolution procedures. These extracted elements are then categorized and structured, allowing for easier review, comparison, and analysis. This is particularly useful during due diligence, compliance checks, or contract negotiations, where businesses need to evaluate large volumes of agreements quickly.

NLP also supports risk identification in documentation. By analyzing the language used in contracts, NLP tools can flag potentially risky terms or deviations from standard contractual language. For example, if a supplier contract omits standard liability limitations or contains unusually broad warranty terms, NLP algorithms can detect these issues by comparing the document to a repository of precedent agreements or pre-approved templates. This allows organizations to assess risk and maintain contract compliance with internal policies or regulatory requirements.

Another application is in contract comparison and version control. When multiple drafts of a contract are exchanged, it can be challenging to track subtle changes. NLP tools can compare different versions of a document, highlighting additions, deletions, and language changes that may affect legal or financial obligations. This reduces the risk of oversight and ensures that key changes are appropriately reviewed by legal or accounting teams.

In regulatory and financial reporting, NLP is used to analyze narrative disclosures within contracts, such as revenue recognition criteria, lease terms, or performance obligations. This is particularly valuable for complying with complex standards like IFRS 15 or ASC 606, which require a detailed understanding of contractual terms. NLP tools can extract these data points, enabling auditors or accountants to verify compliance with accounting standards more efficiently.

Furthermore, NLP enhances workflow automation and integration. Extracted contract terms can be linked directly to financial systems, triggering alerts or actions such as payment scheduling, renewal reminders, or compliance reviews. This integration helps ensure that contractual commitments are tracked and honored throughout their lifecycle.

To summarize, NLP transforms contract and documentation reviews from a manual, time-consuming task into an automated, intelligent process. By enabling clause extraction, risk identification, version control, and compliance analysis, NLP enhances accuracy, reduces costs, and improves the efficiency of legal and financial operations.

Taxation and AI

There are several areas within the field of taxation where AI may be applied. As noted in the following pages, these applications include the preparation of tax returns, discrepancy identification, and the analysis of indirect taxes.

AI in Tax Compliance and Planning

In tax compliance, AI is used to streamline the preparation, review, and filing of tax returns. Natural language processing tools can extract relevant tax data from a variety of sources, including invoices, financial statements, and contracts. Machine learning algorithms are then used to cross-check this information against applicable tax laws and identify potential discrepancies or red flags. For example, AI can flag inconsistencies in VAT filings or determine if a transaction may violate transfer pricing rules. This level of precision reduces the risk of audits, penalties, and reputational damage, while significantly decreasing the time and cost associated with manual tax return processes.

AI also supports real-time monitoring and forecasting of tax positions. Through continuous analysis of transactional data, AI systems can alert tax departments to issues as they arise, rather than after the fact. This proactive approach is especially valuable for multinational corporations, which must navigate complex, multi-jurisdictional tax environments. AI tools can help companies monitor cross-border transactions and ensure that they remain in compliance with the latest international tax standards.

In the area of tax planning, AI enhances strategic decision-making by simulating the tax impact of various financial scenarios. For instance, businesses can use AI to model the tax consequences of mergers and acquisitions, changes in corporate structure, or shifts in operational geography. AI tools can evaluate multiple scenarios in seconds and provide recommendations that optimize tax outcomes while remaining compliant with legal requirements. This allows businesses to make proactive adjustments and capitalize on tax-saving opportunities.

In addition, AI can assist in identifying tax credits and incentives that might otherwise be overlooked. By scanning through thousands of government programs and correlating them with company-specific activities and expenditures, AI systems can uncover potential savings. This is particularly beneficial in industries like manufacturing, technology, or renewable energy, where numerous incentive programs exist.

Despite its advantages, the implementation of AI in tax functions requires careful oversight. The effectiveness of AI tools depends on the quality of the data and the sophistication of the algorithms used. Tax departments must also ensure transparency and auditability of AI decisions, especially when dealing with regulators. As such, collaboration between tax professionals, data scientists, and legal experts is essential to maximize the benefits of AI while maintaining regulatory compliance.

In conclusion, AI enhances both tax compliance and planning by increasing efficiency, accuracy, and strategic insight. It allows businesses to automate routine tasks, anticipate tax obligations, and make informed decisions that align with both their financial goals and tax laws.

How AI Handles Complex Tax Codes and Jurisdictions

Artificial intelligence is increasingly being leveraged to manage the complexities of diverse tax codes and multi-jurisdictional regulations. With tax laws constantly evolving and varying significantly across countries, states, and municipalities, businesses face significant challenges in remaining compliant. AI helps alleviate this burden by processing and interpreting large volumes of regulatory data, identifying relevant rules, and applying them accurately to specific financial activities.

One of the key strengths of AI in this context is its ability to analyze unstructured data from legal texts, tax codes, regulatory updates, and case law. Using natural language processing, AI systems can extract meaning from complex legal language, convert it into structured data, and align it with internal business transactions. For example, a global corporation operating in dozens of countries might need to understand the tax treatment of employee benefits in each jurisdiction. AI can parse the regulatory requirements for each region and ensure correct application in payroll systems.

Machine learning further enhances the AI system's capability by identifying patterns in past compliance activities and regulatory responses. These algorithms can learn from historical filings, audits, and rulings to anticipate tax authority behavior or flag potential issues. As tax environments change, AI models are retrained using updated data, ensuring that they stay current with new legislation, such as digital services taxes or carbon-related levies.

Another critical application is cross-jurisdictional tax calculation and reporting. AI can simultaneously apply multiple tax codes to a single transaction, especially for businesses engaged in international trade. For instance, when a company ships goods from Germany to Brazil via a U.S. subsidiary, AI systems can analyze the tax obligations in all three jurisdictions—including value-added tax (VAT), customs duties, withholding taxes, and transfer pricing requirements—ensuring accurate reporting and minimizing compliance risk.

AI also assists with tax provision calculations under accounting standards such as IFRS and U.S. GAAP. It can model deferred tax liabilities and assets based on differences between accounting income and taxable income across jurisdictions. This is particularly valuable for multinational firms that must comply with both local statutory tax rules and global financial reporting requirements.

Further, AI supports tax compliance in areas with frequent regulatory changes. Tax authorities often issue clarifications, amendments, or guidance notes that require quick adaptation. AI-enabled systems monitor these regulatory changes in real-time, map them to internal tax positions, and generate alerts for potential impact. This dynamic capability helps businesses respond proactively, avoiding penalties and ensuring continuous compliance.

While AI does not replace tax professionals, it allows them to focus on high-value analysis and strategic decision-making rather than routine data processing. The technology can act as a co-pilot—scanning thousands of pages of legislation, identifying relevant clauses, and even suggesting interpretations based on previous rulings.

In summary, AI handles complex tax codes and jurisdictions by combining natural language processing, machine learning, and real-time data processing to interpret, apply, and adapt to varying tax rules. Its ability to manage this complexity at scale reduces errors, improves efficiency, and supports strategic compliance.

Using AI for Indirect Taxes Analysis

Artificial intelligence can enhance the analysis and management of indirect taxes, such as VAT and Goods and Services Tax (GST). These forms of taxation are particularly complex due to their transactional nature, jurisdictional variations, frequent rule changes, and heavy documentation requirements. AI offers a powerful solution by automating tax determination, improving compliance accuracy, and enabling data-driven decision-making for businesses operating across multiple tax regimes.

Indirect tax compliance requires businesses to accurately apply tax rates and rules to a high volume of transactions in real-time. AI, through machine learning algorithms, can learn from historical data to identify correct tax treatments for different transaction types. It can evaluate variables such as product classifications, customer and supplier locations, invoice terms, and jurisdictional rules to determine whether VAT/GST should be applied, at what rate, and whether the tax is recoverable. This drastically reduces manual errors and the risk of non-compliance, especially in cross-border transactions where rules are often inconsistent.

Natural language processing enhances AI's ability to interpret tax laws, government guidance, and updates published in legal and regulatory texts. This allows AI systems to continuously update their rule engines as tax codes evolve. For example, if a country introduces new VAT exemptions or modifies tax thresholds, the AI system can incorporate these changes almost immediately and apply them to future transactions. This reduces the lag between regulatory updates and internal compliance adjustments.

One of the most impactful uses of AI in VAT/GST analysis is anomaly detection. AI tools can analyze millions of transactions and detect irregularities, such as duplicate entries, incorrect tax coding, or tax amounts that deviate from the norm. These insights allow tax teams to perform targeted audits and remediations rather than relying solely on random sampling. For example, if a supplier consistently charges VAT at an incorrect rate, AI can flag this behavior for further investigation, helping prevent the overpayment or underpayment of taxes.

AI also improves the efficiency of VAT/GST reclaim processes. For multinational businesses, reclaiming VAT from foreign jurisdictions can be burdensome, requiring thorough documentation and justification. AI systems can automatically collect, verify, and categorize invoices and receipts to determine eligibility for recovery. They can then generate supporting documentation in the correct format for local authorities, streamlining the reclaim process and accelerating cash flow.

Furthermore, AI enables better strategic planning through VAT/GST analytics. By aggregating and analyzing indirect tax data across regions and product lines, AI can reveal patterns and trends that may indicate inefficiencies or compliance risks. Businesses can use this information to restructure supply chains, optimize invoicing practices, or explore tax incentives that reduce overall tax exposure.

In conclusion, AI plays a key role in the management of indirect taxes by improving accuracy, reducing compliance costs, and providing usable insights. From real-time tax determination and rule interpretation to anomaly detection and strategic planning, AI allows businesses to handle VAT/GST complexities with greater confidence and efficiency.

AI-Powered Decision Support Systems

AI may prove to be exceedingly useful in the area of decision support, since it can be used to develop prescriptive analytics for budgeting, as well as the real-time preparation of dashboards that can keep managers up-to-date on a variety of key performance metrics.

Dashboards and Real-Time Reporting

Artificial intelligence is significantly transforming the design and functionality of dashboards and real-time reporting in finance, accounting, and business operations. Traditionally, dashboards were static tools that relied on manually curated data and pre-set templates. Today, with the integration of AI, dashboards have become dynamic, intelligent platforms capable of real-time analysis, predictive insights, and automated decision support, all of which help businesses respond faster and more effectively to emerging trends and risks.

One of the primary benefits of AI in dashboards is its ability to automate data aggregation from multiple sources, including enterprise resource planning systems, customer relationship management platforms, and external market feeds. AI algorithms process this data continuously and update the dashboard in real-time, ensuring that users always have access to the most current and relevant information. This automation reduces human error and significantly cuts down the time needed to generate accurate reports.

Machine learning enhances dashboards by identifying patterns and correlations in large datasets that may not be immediately apparent to human users. These insights are then visualized on the dashboard through intuitive charts, graphs, and alerts. For example, an AI-enabled dashboard in an accounting department might flag an unusual spike in accounts payable or a decline in gross margins, offering early warnings of potential fraud, operational issues, or market shifts. This proactive capability transforms dashboards from passive data displays into active monitoring tools.

AI also supports natural language processing features within dashboards, allowing users to interact with the system through voice or text queries. Instead of navigating complex menus or filtering data manually, a user can simply ask, "What were the sales figures for the Northeast region last quarter?" and receive a visualized response instantly. This conversational interface makes data more accessible to non-technical users, broadening the dashboard's usability across the organization.

Real-time reporting is another area where AI brings tremendous value. Traditional reporting cycles often suffer from delays due to manual data collection and reconciliation. With AI, reports can be generated automatically as soon as new data is available. AI-driven systems can also personalize reports for different stakeholders by understanding their roles and preferences. A CFO might receive a report focused on profitability and risk metrics, while an operations manager may see a version centered on supply chain efficiency and resource utilization.

Predictive analytics is an advanced feature that AI brings to dashboards and reporting. By analyzing historical data, AI models can forecast future trends, such as expected revenue, customer churn, or inventory shortages. These predictive insights allow organizations to plan more effectively and make informed strategic decisions.

In short, AI enhances dashboards and real-time reporting by automating data integration, enabling predictive analytics, improving data visualization, and personalizing user experiences. These capabilities help organizations shift from reactive to proactive management, increase efficiency, and support data-driven decision-making at all levels.

How AI is Integrated into an ERP System

Artificial intelligence can be integrated into an enterprise resource planning (ERP) system to enhance automation, decision-making, and operational efficiency across various business functions. Integration typically involves linking AI algorithms with ERP databases and workflows through APIs[1] or embedded AI modules offered by ERP vendors. Cloud-based ERP platforms are especially conducive to AI integration, offering scalable computing power and real-time data accessibility.

The Use of Prescriptive Analytics for Budgeting and Resource Allocation

Artificial intelligence is reshaping prescriptive analytics, particularly in the areas of budgeting and resource allocation, by moving beyond traditional forecasting to provide data-driven recommendations on optimal actions. Prescriptive analytics not only identifies what *will* happen but also suggests what should be done in response. AI enhances this process by integrating vast amounts of data, identifying complex patterns, and running simulations that help organizations make better financial and operational decisions.

Note: *Prescriptive analytics* is a form of data analytics that goes beyond describing what has happened (descriptive analytics) and predicting what might happen (predictive analytics) to recommend specific actions to achieve desired outcomes.

In budgeting, AI-powered prescriptive analytics enables organizations to move from static annual plans to more dynamic and adaptive budgeting models. Traditional budgeting often relies on historical data and manual inputs, which can result in outdated assumptions and inefficient capital deployment. AI, on the other hand, continuously processes real-time data, such as sales performance, market trends, and operational metrics, and recommends how budgets should be adjusted in response to current and

---

[1] An API (Application Programming Interface) is a set of rules and protocols that allows different software applications to communicate and share data with each other. It acts as a bridge, enabling systems to interact without needing to understand each other's internal workings.

projected conditions. For example, if an AI model detects that a certain product line is outperforming forecasts due to rising demand, it can recommend reallocating marketing funds to that product or ramping up production capacity.

AI also improves resource allocation by modeling various scenarios and recommending the most efficient use of financial, human, and material resources. Through techniques such as *reinforcement learning* and *optimization algorithms*, AI can simulate the impact of different decisions under varying conditions. For instance, a healthcare organization might use AI to determine the optimal staffing levels across departments during flu season, balancing cost constraints with service delivery requirements. Similarly, a manufacturing company can leverage AI to recommend investments in machinery or labor depending on changes in demand, supply chain constraints, or energy costs.

In addition, AI's ability to analyze external factors, such as market conditions, regulatory changes, and competitor behavior, further strengthens prescriptive analytics. By incorporating both internal performance data and external variables, AI systems provide a holistic view that helps organizations avoid over- or under-allocating resources. For example, in response to geopolitical developments or inflation trends, AI may suggest revisiting supplier contracts or shifting inventory strategies.

Furthermore, AI ensures that prescriptive analytics is ongoing, not just a once-a-year event. As new data flows in, AI models continuously update recommendations, allowing businesses to stay agile. This is especially valuable during periods of volatility, such as economic downturns or supply chain disruptions, when the rapid reallocation of resources can mitigate risks and seize emerging opportunities.

In summary, AI significantly enhances prescriptive analytics in budgeting and resource allocation by providing intelligent, actionable recommendations grounded in real-time and predictive data. It allows businesses to make faster, more informed, and more effective decisions, ultimately leading to improved financial performance and operational efficiency.

Data Governance and Ethical Considerations

While the use of AI appears to be quite promising, one must also be aware of the potential downsides, such as skewed results that are due to poor data integrity. This can result in notable levels of model bias. Both concepts are discussed in the following pages.

The Importance of Data Integrity and Quality in AI

In the field of accounting, the integrity and quality of data are foundational to the successful implementation and performance of artificial intelligence systems. Accounting relies heavily on accurate, consistent, and timely information to support financial reporting, compliance, auditing, forecasting, and decision-making. When AI is integrated into accounting workflows, such as for automating transaction processing, conducting predictive analytics, or detecting anomalies, the outputs of these systems are only as reliable as the data on which they are trained and operate.

Examples of AI-Powered Decision Support Systems

Here are several examples of AI-driven financial planning tools commonly used by businesses:

Datarails. Designed for small and mid-sized businesses, it combines AI with Excel-based environments to automate data consolidation, forecasting, and dashboard creation.

Fathom. Focuses on visual financial analysis and forecasting, using AI to create interactive dashboards and cash flow projections based on accounting system integrations.

Kepion. Offers AI-enhanced planning and budgeting tools with predictive modeling and business rule automation, often used for sales and operational planning.

Oracle Cloud EPM (Enterprise Performance Management). Uses AI and advanced analytics to provide predictive planning, data visualization, and real-time strategy modeling for large enterprises.

Planful. Uses AI to automate budgeting, forecasting, and reporting, offering predictive insights and real-time collaboration across departments.

Prophix. Employs AI and natural language processing to streamline financial planning, support cash flow forecasting, and analyze financial performance trends.

Vena Solutions. Integrates AI to enhance financial modeling, scenario planning, and variance analysis, while providing smart recommendations based on historical and real-time data.

Workday Adaptive Planning. Incorporates machine learning for dynamic forecasting, automated anomaly detection, and what-if scenario analysis.

Therefore, data integrity and quality are critical for ensuring that AI delivers meaningful insights.

Data integrity refers to the accuracy, consistency, and reliability of data throughout its lifecycle. In an AI context, maintaining data integrity means ensuring that accounting data is not corrupted or altered as it moves through systems. For instance, if journal entries are changed without proper controls or audit trails, the AI models that rely on this data may generate flawed predictions or misidentify fraudulent activities. This could result in financial misstatements, regulatory non-compliance, or the loss of stakeholder trust.

Data quality, on the other hand, encompasses dimensions such as accuracy, completeness, timeliness, relevance, and validity. AI models require high-quality historical and real-time accounting data to function effectively. For example, if a machine learning model is being used to forecast cash flows or detect expense anomalies, it must be trained on data that accurately reflects real-world conditions. Missing fields, duplicated entries, or outdated information can lead to poor model performance and incorrect conclusions, potentially harming business outcomes.

In accounting, data is often aggregated from multiple sources, such as enterprise resource planning systems, invoices, bank feeds, tax filings, and audit trails. If the data from these sources is not standardized and reconciled, AI systems may struggle to interpret and process it. For example, inconsistent naming conventions for accounts or departments can hinder the model's ability to identify trends or discrepancies. Ensuring data consistency across systems and departments is essential to maintaining a trustworthy AI environment.

Furthermore, regulatory frameworks such as GAAP and IFRS impose stringent requirements on the accuracy and verifiability of financial records. AI applications must align with these standards, which can only be achieved if the data inputs meet the required quality and integrity thresholds. Failure to do so could expose organizations to compliance risks and legal penalties.

In conclusion, for AI to truly enhance accounting processes, data integrity and quality must be prioritized at every stage, from data collection and cleansing to model training and deployment. Organizations should implement robust data governance policies, continuous data validation processes, and internal controls to uphold these standards.

Bias in AI Models

Bias in AI models is a significant concern, particularly when these models are applied to accounting functions. Bias occurs when an AI system produces systematically prejudiced outcomes due to skewed data, flawed assumptions, or imbalanced training processes. In accounting, where accuracy, objectivity, and compliance are paramount, biased AI models can lead to serious misjudgments, legal risks, and ethical concerns.

Bias in AI can originate from several sources. One of the most common is training data bias. If the historical data used to train an AI model reflects previous human errors, inefficiencies, or discriminatory practices, the model will learn and potentially replicate these patterns. For example, if an AI system is trained on expense reports that have historically flagged certain departments or regions more often, it may continue to do so even when current data does not support such a pattern, thereby perpetuating systemic bias.

Algorithmic bias is another concern. This occurs when a model's design, such as the features selected or the way the algorithm weighs certain inputs, unintentionally favors or disadvantages specific outcomes. In accounting, this could manifest in areas such as risk scoring for audits, where certain types of transactions or entities are overrepresented in red-flag categories. This could lead to the misallocation of audit resources, overlooked anomalies, or increased scrutiny on particular vendors or business units without proper justification.

The impact of bias in accounting AI applications can be substantial. In financial forecasting, for instance, a biased model may produce forecasts that favor conservative or aggressive assumptions based on skewed historical performance, leading to inaccurate budgets or misguided investment decisions. In fraud detection, biased models may fail to recognize fraud in less-represented scenarios or over-flag normal activity as suspicious. This not only reduces trust in the system but can also divert attention from actual risks.

Moreover, bias undermines regulatory compliance. Accounting is a highly regulated field, and financial decisions must be supported by evidence-based, fair, and unbiased processes. If AI systems used in compliance monitoring, tax planning, or financial reporting exhibit bias, they could contribute to non-compliance with laws such as the Sarbanes-Oxley Act or violate ethical codes governing accountants. This could result in penalties, reputational damage, or legal liabilities.

To mitigate AI bias in accounting, several practices should be adopted. These include diversifying training data, regularly auditing models, and implementing explainability mechanisms that allow users to understand how decisions are made. Transparent model development and validation processes are critical, as is the inclusion of domain experts, such as accountants and auditors, in model oversight. Additionally, organizations should enforce robust governance frameworks that include ethical reviews of AI applications and continuous monitoring for biased behavior.

In conclusion, while AI offers powerful tools to enhance accounting operations, bias in AI models poses a significant risk to accuracy, fairness, and compliance. Accountants must approach AI with a critical eye, ensuring that the models they deploy are transparent, equitable, and subject to ongoing review to uphold the integrity of financial decision-making.

The Ethical Use of Customer and Financial Data

The ethical use of customer and financial data in accounting is a critical concern in today's data-driven environment. Accountants are entrusted with sensitive information, such as client identities, transaction histories, tax records, and proprietary business data, that must be handled with the highest standards of confidentiality. As accounting systems become increasingly digital and integrated with advanced technologies like artificial intelligence, the potential for misuse or mishandling of this data has grown, raising important ethical considerations.

Confidentiality is a cornerstone of ethical accounting. Professional codes of conduct emphasize the duty to protect client information from unauthorized disclosure. This means accountants must take proactive steps to secure both physical and digital records, restrict access only to authorized personnel, and implement safeguards like encryption and secure authentication. Even inadvertent leaks, such as sending reports to the wrong recipient or failing to anonymize data, can breach ethical duties and legal regulations.

Consent and transparency are also essential. Customers and stakeholders should be clearly informed about how their data is collected, stored, and used. In accounting, this applies when data is shared with third-party software providers, outsourced services, or during financial audits and due diligence processes. Ethical accounting practices require that individuals are aware of what data is being used and for what purpose, and that their consent is obtained when necessary. Ambiguous or hidden data use, especially for purposes such as data mining or AI model training, can violate both ethical norms and consumer trust.

Accuracy and integrity in data handling are fundamental to ensuring fair outcomes. Inaccurate financial data, whether resulting from human error or deliberate manipulation, can lead to incorrect reporting, misinformed decisions, and financial harm. Ethical accountants must verify data integrity, avoid misleading representations, and promptly correct known errors. Furthermore, when using financial data in AI or analytics applications, there is a responsibility to prevent misapplication, such as drawing misleading conclusions from incomplete or biased data sets.

Another dimension of ethical data use is limiting data to its intended purpose. Financial data collected for preparing tax returns or generating financial statements should not be repurposed for marketing, profiling, or unrelated business activities without proper justification and consent. Ethical boundaries help prevent misuse and ensure that accountants respect client expectations and privacy.

Finally, accountability and oversight are crucial. Firms must implement governance frameworks that monitor data usage, ensure compliance with ethical and legal standards, and respond to breaches or complaints. Employees should be trained in ethical data practices and encouraged to report suspicious behavior without fear of retaliation.

In conclusion, the ethical use of customer and financial data in accounting demands a culture of trust, transparency, and accountability. As technology advances and data becomes more accessible, ethical vigilance is essential to protecting customer interests, maintaining professional integrity, and ensuring that financial data serves its intended role.

AI Implementations

It can be difficult to implement a workable AI solution, since it is usually only available within the larger ERP systems; accountants will need to bolt AI applications onto their existing accounting systems (at least until the smaller software providers integrate AI into their offerings). Consequently, the following discussions of implementation strategy and vendor selection may prove useful.

Implementation Strategy for AI in Accounting

Assessing an accounting department's readiness for artificial intelligence and planning its integration with existing systems requires a strategic, multi-phase approach. Successful AI adoption hinges not only on technology but also on organizational culture, data infrastructure, and alignment with accounting objectives. The process can be broken down into the following key steps, each critical to ensuring that AI enhances operations without disrupting core financial responsibilities:

1. *Conduct a readiness assessment.* The first step is to evaluate the department's current state across people, processes, and technology. This involves assessing the digital maturity of the accounting function, including its use of automation, data analytics, and cloud-based systems. Surveys and interviews can help gauge staff attitudes toward AI, identify skills gaps, and uncover resistance to change. Departments should also assess their existing workflows to identify repetitive, rule-based tasks that are strong candidates for AI automation, such as invoice processing, reconciliations, or expense categorization.

2. *Audit data quality and infrastructure.* AI models rely heavily on large volumes of accurate, structured data. Therefore, organizations must review their data repositories to assess completeness, consistency, and cleanliness. Disparate systems or manual processes that produce fragmented or siloed data can hinder AI success. A thorough audit should evaluate whether data from ERP systems, financial records, payroll, and procurement systems is integrated and accessible. Where necessary, data governance protocols should be developed to improve data management and ensure compliance with privacy regulations.

3. *Define AI use cases and objectives.* With a clear understanding of current capabilities, departments must then identify and prioritize AI use cases that align with strategic goals. Examples include using AI for predictive cash flow forecasting, fraud detection, or continuous auditing. Each use case should include measurable objectives, such as reducing month-end close time or improving forecasting accuracy, and a cost-benefit analysis to support the investment. It is important to focus on use cases that can deliver early wins, building momentum and confidence in the technology.

4. *Evaluate technology compatibility.* Next, assess the compatibility of AI tools with existing accounting software and IT infrastructure. This includes determining whether AI solutions can integrate with the current ERP system, whether APIs are available for data sharing, and whether the organization's IT environment can support scalable AI computing requirements. Interoperability is crucial to avoid data silos and ensure seamless workflow integration.

5. *Develop an AI integration plan.* An implementation roadmap should be created to guide the integration process. This includes defining timelines, allocating budgets, selecting vendors, and identifying pilot projects. The plan should include phases for prototyping, testing, scaling, and evaluating performance. Risk management strategies should also be included to address issues such as model bias, data breaches, or system errors.

6. *Train staff and foster change management.* AI implementation will change how accountants work, so training is essential. Employees should be educated on AI concepts, the rationale behind implementation, and how it supports rather than replaces their roles. Involving staff early and addressing concerns helps promote adoption and minimize resistance.

In conclusion, a structured approach to assessing readiness and planning integration ensures that AI initiatives are tailored, strategic, and aligned with the accounting department's operational and compliance goals.

Evaluating AI Vendors and Software Platforms

Evaluating vendors and software platforms is a critical step when acquiring AI tools for the accounting department. The decision must be driven by both technological capability and alignment with business needs, particularly the stringent accuracy, compliance, and security requirements of accounting functions. A structured evaluation process ensures that the selected AI solution enhances efficiency, accuracy, and decision-making without introducing unnecessary risk or complexity. Therefore, consider using the following evaluation activities:

1. *Identify functional requirements.* Begin by defining the specific accounting functions the AI tool should support. These may include automating accounts payable, detecting fraud, forecasting cash flows, performing reconciliations, or generating real-time financial reports. Clearly outlining these requirements helps in shortlisting vendors who specialize in those areas. The ideal software should align with your department's pain points and deliver measurable value through enhanced speed, accuracy, or insights.

2. *Assess integration capabilities.* One of the most crucial considerations is how well the AI platform integrates with existing systems such as ERP software, the general ledger, and payroll. Evaluate whether the tool supports open APIs, real-time data exchange, and seamless interoperability. A solution that requires excessive customization to connect with your existing infrastructure may introduce delays and long-term costs. Request technical documentation or demonstrations to confirm compatibility.

3. *Evaluate data security and compliance.* Accounting departments handle highly sensitive financial and customer data. Therefore, it is essential to evaluate the vendor's data security practices. Ensure that the platform complies with relevant regulations such as the General Data Protection Regulation, SOX, or the California Consumer Privacy Act. Look for features such as encryption, role-based access controls, secure audit trails, and compliance certifications like SOC 2 or ISO 27001.

4. *Review AI transparency and accuracy.* Not all AI tools provide the same level of transparency. Prioritize platforms that offer explainable AI, allowing users to understand how decisions are made and models are trained. This is especially important in accounting, where outputs must often be justified to auditors and regulators. Ask vendors for accuracy metrics, error rates, and how their systems handle exceptions. Also, inquire about bias mitigation strategies and data training protocols.

5. *Examine vendor reputation.* Assess the vendor's experience, client base, and industry reputation. Look for case studies, client testimonials, and third-party reviews specific to the accounting sector. It is beneficial to engage with vendors who have a proven track record of successful AI implementations in similar environments. Additionally, review the quality of customer support, evaluating the availability of onboarding assistance, user training, technical support, and post-deployment maintenance.

6. *Consider cost, scalability, and ROI.* The total cost of ownership goes beyond the initial license fee. Evaluate subscription pricing, implementation fees, training costs, and support charges. Also consider the platform's scalability; can it handle increased data volumes and expand to other departments as needed? Conduct a cost-benefit analysis to estimate the return on investment based on projected efficiency gains and risk reduction.

In conclusion, evaluating AI vendors requires a comprehensive approach that balances functionality, integration, security, transparency, and support. By conducting a thorough evaluation, organizations can ensure that they select a solution that delivers tangible improvements while supporting compliance and maintaining trust in financial reporting.

The Future of AI in Accounting

The integration of artificial intelligence into the accounting profession is transforming the landscape of financial operations, compliance, and decision-making. As AI technologies advance, they are increasingly moving beyond routine automation into sophisticated realms such as cognitive computing and autonomous accounting. These innovations are reshaping not only how accounting tasks are performed but also the roles, responsibilities, and required skill sets of accountants. This evolution presents both opportunities and challenges as the profession adapts to a data-rich, technology-driven environment. The following issues can be expected to impact the accounting profession:

- *Cognitive computing.* Cognitive computing refers to AI systems that simulate human thought processes through natural language processing, machine learning, and data mining. In accounting, cognitive computing enables systems to analyze unstructured data—such as contracts, invoices, and emails—draw conclusions, and provide actionable recommendations. For example, cognitive AI can interpret lease agreements to extract relevant accounting data for compliance with standards like ASC 842, or it can review email communications for indications of financial fraud. This represents a significant leap from traditional rule-based automation, which is limited to structured data and predefined rules. Cognitive computing enables real-time decision support, assisting accountants with complex tasks like financial forecasting, compliance analysis, and strategic planning. These systems can continuously learn from new data and user behavior, enhancing their accuracy and value over time.

- *Autonomous accounting.* Autonomous accounting refers to the use of AI to create self-operating systems that can manage the end-to-end accounting lifecycle with minimal human intervention. This includes real-time data collection, classification, reconciliation, anomaly detection, and financial reporting. Autonomous systems use a blend of AI components: robotic process automation to perform repetitive tasks, machine learning to refine classifications and predictions, and natural language generation to produce narratives for financial reports. Over time, autonomous systems can reduce the close cycle from weeks to days or even hours, enhancing decision-making speed and financial agility. As these systems mature, accountants will shift from performing manual tasks to supervising and validating automated workflows. This transition promotes higher value work such as analysis, interpretation, and advising.

- *Predictive and prescriptive analytics*. AI-driven predictive analytics uses historical data to forecast future outcomes, such as cash flow trends, revenue projections, or risk exposures. Prescriptive analytics goes a step further by recommending actions to achieve desired financial results or to mitigate risks. In the future, these tools will become more embedded in accounting software, enabling real-time scenario modeling and strategic insight. For instance, AI can simulate the financial impact of changing supplier terms or tax policies, providing executives with immediate recommendations. This capability not only supports faster, evidence-based decision-making but also aligns accounting more closely with strategic business planning.

- *Collaborative human-AI workflows*. Rather than replacing accountants, AI is poised to augment their capabilities. Human judgment, skepticism, and professional ethics remain irreplaceable, especially in ambiguous or novel situations where AI lacks context. Future accounting departments will operate in a collaborative model, where AI handles high-volume, data-intensive tasks, while human professionals provide oversight, contextual interpretation, and ethical reasoning. This synergy will enhance productivity, reduce errors, and allow accountants to deliver more value-added services.

- *Audit impact*. AI is revolutionizing audit processes through continuous auditing and anomaly detection. Rather than relying on periodic sampling, AI systems can monitor transactions in real time, identifying irregularities as they occur. Cognitive tools can read contracts, extract terms, and verify compliance automatically, reducing the need for manual document review. AI also facilitates risk-based auditing, where resources are concentrated on high-risk areas identified by predictive algorithms. As a result, auditors will need to develop new competencies in data science, audit analytics, and AI oversight. Their role will evolve to include validating AI-driven audit tools and ensuring that automated processes meet regulatory and ethical standards.

- *Ethical considerations*. As AI becomes more central to accounting, ethical considerations and governance frameworks will become increasingly important. Bias in AI models, the misuse of financial data, and lack of transparency in decision-making are significant risks. Future accountants will be responsible not only for producing accurate financial results but also for ensuring that AI tools are used responsibly. This includes establishing data governance policies, auditing AI models for fairness and accuracy, and maintaining compliance with privacy laws such as GDPR and CCPA.

As AI takes over transactional and repetitive tasks, the role of accountants is undergoing a significant transformation. Future accountants will act more as analysts, strategists, and advisors than bookkeepers or data entry clerks. Key shifts in roles include the following:

- *From preparer to interpreter*. Accountants will focus more on interpreting AI-generated outputs, verifying their accuracy, and explaining the implications to stakeholders.

- *From compliance to strategy.* With AI ensuring ongoing compliance and data accuracy, accountants will contribute more to strategic decision-making, including scenario planning and risk assessment.
- *From technician to technologist.* Proficiency in data analytics tools, AI systems, and business intelligence platforms will become essential. Accountants must understand how AI models function, their limitations, and how to validate their results.
- *From reactive to proactive.* AI allows for real-time monitoring and forecasting, enabling accountants to proactively identify issues before they materialize, such as liquidity risks or expense overruns.

This evolution will require a redefinition of accounting education and training, with greater emphasis on data literacy, AI ethics, cybersecurity, and critical thinking.

In short, the future impact of AI on accounting will likely be marked by the convergence of emerging technologies and evolving professional roles. Cognitive computing and autonomous accounting will redefine how financial information is captured, analyzed, and reported, thereby enabling unprecedented efficiency and insight. However, these advances also demand a transformation in skills, mindsets, and ethical frameworks.

Summary

This manual has provided a comprehensive exploration of how artificial intelligence is revolutionizing the accounting profession. It introduced key AI concepts, such as machine learning, natural language processing, and cognitive computing, and demonstrated their practical applications in automating data entry, invoice processing, reconciliations, fraud detection, and predictive analytics. The manual also highlighted case studies from major companies like Microsoft and Coca-Cola, showing real-world implementations of AI in financial reporting, audits, and risk management. Additionally, it addressed ethical and regulatory concerns, including data integrity, bias, privacy, and auditability. In short, *AI for Accountants* prepares accountants to adapt to evolving roles and harness AI for strategic insight, accuracy, and operational efficiency.

Glossary

A

Algorithm. A step-by-step set of rules or instructions given to an AI system or computer to perform a specific task or solve a problem.

Algorithmic bias. When a machine learning model produces systematically unfair outcomes due to biased training data, flawed assumptions, or unequal representation.

Anomaly detection. The process of identifying data points, events, or patterns that deviate significantly from the norm, often indicating errors or unusual behavior.

Artificial intelligence. The broad field of computer science focused on creating systems capable of performing tasks that typically require human intelligence. These tasks include reasoning, learning, problem-solving, perception, and language understanding.

B

Bias. Systematic errors in AI outcomes caused by flawed data, assumptions, or algorithms, often resulting in unfair or inaccurate results.

C

Cognitive computing. A branch of AI that simulates human thought processes by using machine learning, natural language processing, and pattern recognition to solve complex problems.

Computer vision. A field of AI that enables machines to interpret and understand visual information from the world, such as images and videos.

D

Data integrity. The accuracy, consistency, and reliability of data throughout its lifecycle.

Data quality. The accuracy, completeness, consistency, and reliability of data.

Deep learning. A specialized branch of machine learning that uses multi-layered neural networks to model complex patterns in large datasets. Deep learning is especially effective in areas such as image recognition, speech processing, and natural language understanding.

I

Intelligent sampling. The strategic selection of data subsets that best represent the entire dataset to improve model efficiency and accuracy while reducing computational costs.

M

Machine learning. A subset of AI that enables computers to learn from data without being explicitly programmed. Machine learning algorithms use statistical techniques to identify patterns and improve their performance on a task over time.

N

Natural language generation. The process by which artificial intelligence converts structured data into coherent, human-like text.

Natural language processing. A field of AI that enables machines to understand, interpret, and generate human language. NLP powers applications like chatbots, machine translation, sentiment analysis, and voice-activated assistants.

Neural network. A computational model inspired by the human brain, consisting of layers of interconnected nodes (neurons) that process and transmit information. Neural networks are fundamental to many deep learning systems.

O

Optimization algorithms. Mathematical methods used in AI to adjust model parameters and minimize or maximize a specific objective function for improved performance.

P

Pattern recognition. The process by which AI systems identify and classify regularities or trends in data to make predictions or decisions.

Predictive analytics. The use of historical data, statistical algorithms, and machine learning techniques to forecast future outcomes and trends.

Preprocessing. The preparation and transformation of raw data into a clean, structured format suitable for training and evaluating machine learning models.

Prescriptive analytics. The use of data, algorithms, and machine learning to recommend optimal actions and decision paths to achieve desired outcomes.

R

Reinforcement learning. A type of machine learning where an agent learns to make decisions by performing actions in an environment and receiving rewards or penalties as feedback.

Robotic process automation. A technology that uses software robots to automate highly repetitive and rule-based tasks within business processes.

S

Semi-structured data. Information that does not reside in a traditional database format but still contains organizational properties, such as tags or markers, that make it easier to analyze.

Structured data. Highly organized information formatted in a way, such as rows and columns, that is easily searchable and analyzable by computers.

Supervised learning. A machine learning approach where the model is trained on labeled data, so it learns to predict outcomes based on new inputs.

T

Time-series data. Sequential observations collected over time, typically used to identify trends, patterns, and seasonal effects.

Training data. The dataset used to teach an AI or machine learning model, enabling it to recognize patterns and make predictions.

U

Unstructured data. Information that lacks a predefined format or organization, making it difficult to analyze using traditional data tools.

Unsupervised learning. A machine learning method in which the model analyzes data without labeled responses, identifying hidden patterns or groupings in the data.

Index

www.ingramcontent.com/pod-product-compliance
Lightning Source LLC
Chambersburg PA
CBHW080353030726
47598CB00009B/2730